The Beaded Kingdom

Change Your Thought Patterns to Improve Your Life

by Renee Heiss

Illustrations by Amy & Angie Bonnett,

J.T. Anglin and Anthony Phillips

The Beaded Kingdom: Change Your Thought Patterns to Improve Your Life

For more information or permission to reproduce selections from this book, please visit the Character Publishing website: www.CharacterPublishing.ORG

Library of Congress Cataloging-in-Publication Data
Heiss, Elizabeth Renee
The Beaded Kingdom: Change Your Thought Patterns to Improve Your Life/written by Renee Heiss

Summary: Change your thoughts. Change your actions. Change your life. It is that easy to be happy. But most people forget that their thoughts control their actions, and their actions control their lives. By using a sensory stimulus, a Beaded Chain, readers will be reminded to stay positive and nurture their mental kingdoms, rather than sabotaging their kingdoms with negativity. *The Beaded Kingdom* shows young people how to categorize their priorities in an imaginary mental kingdom.

[1. Children's - Self Help. 2. Children's - Nonfiction]
ISBN 978-0-9890797-1-6

Library of Congress Control Number: 2013936881

First Edition
Edited by Jerusha Bosarge and Brie Ishee
Design and Illustration Assistance by Angela Tran

*This book is dedicated to all the people I have met
who contributed to the health of my own Beaded Kingdom.
Without them, this book would not have been possible.
-RH*

TABLE OF CONTENTS

What is a Beaded Kingdom?

A Beaded Kingdom is a group of people who understand that their thoughts control their actions and their lives. They wear a beaded necklace or bracelet to remind them of all the ways they can use their thoughts to positively control their actions and their lives. Each bead symbolizes a different way of looking at everyday events. It's as simple as that.

If you already have a beaded chain that you wear frequently, put it on now. If you don't have one, don't worry. You can get one later, or use the directions at the end of this book to make one that will be uniquely yours. Your beaded chain can be a fancy gold chain with charms, a long piece of yarn with homemade beads of paper, or any variety of necklace in between. It can hang low or hug your neck. The material, size, and color of your beaded chain do not matter. All that matters is that you understand that you can change your life when you change the way you think about it. The chain will help to remind you of this.

You can also change the relationships in your life by restructuring how you think about the people in those relationships. Touch your beaded chain frequently to remember that you are a member of *The Beaded Kingdom.* Each bead on your chain represents a concept that helps you understand how your thoughts control your actions, your relationships, and your happiness!

Consider this scenario: Melanie worried about the upcoming chemistry test. She knew she hadn't been paying attention in class and hadn't made time to study. The night before the test, when she was supposed to study, she sprained her ankle and spent most of the evening in the emergency room getting x-rays to make sure it wasn't broken. She never got to study for the test and told herself she simply didn't care whether she passed it or not. She went into school unprepared, took the test, and eventually got a failing grade. Why? Because her thoughts controlled her life. She worried about failing, so she did. Believe it or not, her negative thoughts may have actually controlled her clumsiness. Research has shown that people with positive self-esteem are less clumsy than people with negative self-esteem.

Now consider this scenario: Mario knew he wanted to be a pediatrician one day. He knew that his high school grades would control whether he got into a good college. He told himself he had to pass the chemistry test. He paid attention in class, he did all the homework, and he understood the concepts. The night before the test, he reviewed his notes. The next day, he took the test and got an A+. Why? Was it because he's smarter than Melanie?

NO!

It was because his thoughts controlled his life. He pictured himself passing, so he did. Naturally, picturing yourself passing a test without studying will not lead to the same passing grade. But it was Mario's thoughts about passing that influenced his actions and caused him to study, which eventually helped him to pass his chemistry test. It's a simple process that works nearly every time.

Look anywhere on the Internet for articles about thoughts controlling actions, and you'll find many people who have researched this phenomenon. I won't bore you with the details, but you should know that research has proven the link between thoughts and actions. When you change your thoughts, you change your actions, you change your relationships, and you change your life.

THOUGHTS ARE MAGNETIC

Consider the last time you had a problem that needed your attention. It could have been an argument you had with your parents. It might have been a friend who betrayed you. Maybe you didn't make the team. Whatever your problem was, you thought, and thought, and thought about it. You pulled your ideas together until you either made a mental mountain out of a molehill, or you reconciled your feelings about the problem and got on with your life. Thoughts are magnetic; they pull other thoughts along with them.

Sometimes those thoughts are good, and they pull other good thoughts with them. Sometimes they are emotionally harmful and pull other harmful thoughts with them. You don't pull harmful and good thoughts together. They magnetically oppose each other. That's why you feel so miserable when you have conflicted thoughts – should I, or shouldn't I?

Let's go back to Melanie and Mario. Melanie failed her test. She blamed her teacher for not explaining the work better. She blamed herself for not paying attention in class. She blamed her clumsiness for landing her in the hospital the night before the test. She blamed everybody and everything except what she should have blamed the bad test grade on - her own negative thoughts.

Mario, on the other hand, passed the test. He felt good about the results of his efforts. Then, he let go of that test and moved on to the next test, perhaps in math or history. His positive thoughts about passing the chemistry test attracted other good thoughts about passing other tests in other subjects. His thoughts influenced his ability to pass his tests. The fact that Mario is a more successful student than Melanie is not random. It was controlled by his thoughts, both consciously and subconsciously.

Wishes vs. Thoughts

You've probably heard people utter a variety of wishes as you stroll past the tables in the cafeteria. "I wish I was prettier." "I wish I had more money." "I wish I had a car." "I wish my boyfriend treated me better." And the list could go on and on. Wishing for something does not constitute the positive thoughts that got Mario the high grade. Wishes are mental clouds. They have little substance and contribute little toward your actions. Wishes are unfulfilled thoughts.

So, how can you transform wishes into positive thoughts that actually change things? Through positive thinking about *the road* to your goals. Wishes are the clouds over your road, and only you can control whether you head in a positive direction toward sunnier days or in a negative direction toward an emotional storm. When you say, "I wish I had a job," and then go watch TV, that wish evaporates. However, if you say, "I wish I had a job," and then look through the want-ads, the wish cloud transforms into a positive thought that brings about positive actions that lead you on the road to your job. Those actions will transform your life because you have control over your thoughts. If you tell yourself you are able to get a job, and then you take actions to support that road of thought, you will actually get a job.

Focus Your Thoughts With Laser Accuracy

Whether you call it prayer, meditation, or cocentration, the act of focusing thoughts brings about changes in your actions. Remember those magnetic thoughts? Think about hundreds of positive thoughts coming together on one topic. With all that effort, you will be able to develop a creative solution to any situation.

Think of it this way. In its simplest definition, a laser is a highly concentrated, focused beam of light. It accomplishes much more than your average light bulb, which uses a more diffused light beam. A laser can repair a cataract, print text on paper, and provide a dynamic performance at a concert. Can a light bulb do that?

Most people's thoughts are like that light bulb.

They think shallowly about many different things at once – the movie on Saturday, their jobs, their relationships, and even their futures. People who concentrate their thoughts on one topic at a time achieve so much more than those who broadcast their thoughts about many different topics.

For some people, focusing thoughts is not that easy. People with ADD find themselves easily distracted, unable to focus on one topic for long periods of time. If you are one of those people, how can you train yourself to focus? With a sensory stimulus. When you link your thoughts to a picture, you begin to focus your thoughts on that image. When you touch something continually, you focus your thoughts on that item. When you smell a particular odor, you focus on that fragrance. Sensory stimulation increases the powers of concentration.

Let's go back to Melanie and Mario again. Melanie was pessimistic and thought she would fail the test. She probably did not give herself a sensory stimulus for focusing her very weak positive thoughts about the test. Mario probably carried around his chemistry book on the top of his pile. This reminded him that the test would need his full attention. Mario used the visual stimulus of the chemistry book to focus his positive thoughts on the test. As he reviewed the night before, he might have eaten a peppermint candy.

On the day of the test, he pops another candy in his mouth. The familiar odor reminded him of what he had studied the night before. Maybe he even has a beaded chain that he wears around his neck that he touches occasionally to remind him to think positively about his goals. Mario is successful because he focuses his thoughts using sensory stimulation. You can do that, too, when you wear your beaded chain.

Change Your Mindset

When you wake up in the morning, what is the first thing you think about? Do you think, "Oh well, I guess I'll have to deal with another day?" Or do you think, "Wow! Today will be much better than yesterday!" Or maybe you wake up all excited to begin a new day, only to find out that the day goes downhill fast. The way you think about your life will influence how you react to life's setbacks, disappointments, and wrinkles.

You have a choice. You can either complain about problems, or you can feel gratitude. Gratitude for problems? No. Gratitude for the bounty of good things you find outside of the problem. Mario seems to be doing okay for himself, so let's help Melanie. She failed her test, and she's probably complaining about a number of issues, not all of which are directly related to that test. How can she find something to feel thankful for in the middle of all those problems? With creative thought.

Melanie needs to think about the good things in her life. She might say, "Well, I failed the test, but the good news is that the teacher gave me an opportunity to re-take the test to bring up my grade."

Maybe Melanie complains that she doesn't understand the subject. Instead of complaining about her lack of chemistry knowledge, she can say, "The good news is that I can stay after school on Tuesday afternoons for extra help." When Melanie sees her life as a series of good things that come directly from her problems, her life will begin to improve.

Melanie has changed her mindset from complaint to gratitude through creative thought. When she changed her mindset, she also began to change her actions. Through creative, positive thinking, Melanie improved her grade on her next test.

When she changed her actions, she changed her life. You can, too.

What This Book Won't Do

You won't find lectures in this book on how to live. You won't find me telling you to stay away from drugs, alcohol, and other dangerous acts. You get enough of that advice from teachers, parents, and the media. I won't tell you how to study for your next test or what to do about a cheating boyfriend or girlfriend. I won't even tell you what to think, just how to change your thoughts to improve your life.

I won't lead you to believe that as a result of reading this book and implementing the beaded chain, your life will change overnight. That won't happen. Just as a seed needs to grow gradually to bloom into a beautiful flower, your power of positive thinking will likely start small. Eventually, you'll see the beautiful flower that your life will become. That may take several weeks, or it may take several years. However, when you think positively and act on those positive thoughts, your life will definitely improve.

I also won't tell you about other people's success stories. But when you learn how to use your beaded chain, you'll begin to see patterns. You'll look around at successful people and see that they used one or more of the "beads" in your chain. Then, maybe you'll understand by seeing first-hand how positive thinking can influence your actions and your life.

What This Book Does Do

Through the concepts taught in this book, you will learn how to consider your mind as a mental kingdom. In that kingdom, you have the power to rule your thoughts, as if they were your personal subjects. If you think you have no control over your life, literally think again. The kingdom of your thoughts could very well be the only thing you can control right now. How does that make you feel?

This book will give you a tangible way to remember your personal goals and to use the power of positive thinking to achieve those goals. Each chapter, beginning with this introduction, presents different "beads" of understanding. The beads will help you to remember how to make educated choices based on positive, concentrated thoughts.

This book also shows you how to build your own success story, one step at a time, through positive thinking. As I said before, change is gradual. You may not see an immediate change in your life. However, with constant effort toward positive thinking, you'll find yourself more like Mario and less like Melanie.

You are in total control of your thoughts.
Let them work for you!

Let's Get Started!

At the end of each chapter, you'll find questions to help you decide what each bead on your beaded chain represents. Each person's beaded chain will be unique because each person is an individual with distinctive situations, goals, interests, and abilities. Your beaded chain is yours alone. The answers to the reflection questions are yours alone. Here are the first two beads for your beaded chain. Fill in the answers to understand your interpretation of the bead. You can also draw a picture that represents your interpretation.

 What brings you joy? Who consistently brings you joy? When are you happiest? Where are you happiest?

_____

_____

_____

 When do you feel most relaxed? What kind of music makes you peaceful? What does peace mean to you?

_____

_____

_____

Some people think in pictures, rather than words. If that describes you, then draw a joyful, peaceful picture below. It can be abstract or concrete. You can draw people or simply a series of lines that combine to create a happy image.

CHAPTER ONE – YOUR CASTLE
Freedom

Your castle is the center of your mental kingdom. Look around. What do you see? Do you see servants hard at work keeping your place neat and clean? Those are your positive thoughts. Or maybe you see your servants lounging around, doing nothing to improve your mental castle and letting it get dusty and dirty. Those are your negative thoughts. You have the freedom to choose positive thoughts over negative thoughts all the time.

Castles are usually enormous structures. Your mental castle is big enough to carry every positive thought you have. However, it is also big enough to allow negative thoughts to sneak in. It's your job to hold onto the positive thoughts while blocking the negative ones. To do this, some people keep a daily journal to record their positive and negative thoughts, and then crossing out or even tearing up the negative ones.

How you rule your mental kingdom influences how your kingdom supports your happiness. You can control a kingdom with harsh rules, so the subjects *feel obligated* to obey them. Or you can control a kingdom assertively with fair rules, so the subjects *want* to obey them. What kind of rules do you have for your thoughts? Think about ways you can control your mental kingdom, and your thoughts will help you achieve your goals. Be assertive with your thoughts, allowing positive thoughts to work for you while you push the negative thoughts away. This is *your* castle, and you have the opportunity for complete independence in the way you control your mental kingdom.

Castles use thousands of stones or bricks to create the walls. The bricks and stones are the thoughts you have every day about your life and relationships. Your castle is constantly growing. You'll certainly need to add rooms as your life changes. When you go to college, you'll need a new room for all those thoughts. When you eventually get married, you'll need a new room for those thoughts. If you find yourself with a step-family, you'll likely need a whole new wing. A new boyfriend or girlfriend? Up goes another tower in your castle for that relationship. Each new situation needs a whole new set of positive thoughts to guide it through the tough times. And you will have tough times. But that doesn't mean you need to deal with them in a negative manner. Allow your strong, assertive, independent thoughts to show you the positive way of looking at difficult situations.

Remember to clean your mental castle. Will you leave your thoughts alone? Or will you dust them off occasionally and encourage them to use their magnetic powers to pull in other positive thoughts? I think you know the best answer to that question!

Have you figured out that you have the independence to rule your own mental kingdom, and that you must be assertive with your thoughts in order to maintain strong and positive images? Those are the next two beads in your beaded chain: independence and assertiveness.

When do you feel most independent? What does independence mean to you? How can you train your thoughts to accept independent positive thinking?

_____

_____

_____

_____

Can you tell the difference between being assertive and being aggressive? How can you be assertive with your thoughts so they work for you rather than against you?

_____

_____

_____

_____

In the space below, draw (or paste!) a picture of your castle.

CHAPTER TWO – YOUR CASTLE GARDEN
Goals

icture the garden in your mental kingdom. Is it lush and producing lots of beautiful flowers and delicious fruits and vegetables? Or is it overgrown with weeds, dying a slow death? A producing mental garden comes from careful, thoughtful planning. The overgrown mental garden has had little or no thought or planning put into it.

Let's look at the healthy garden first. A vigorous mental garden begins long before the first sprout. It begins with the overall plan. Do you have a plan? Have you set goals for yourself? Without a plan and goals, your thoughts have no place to focus. Perhaps your plans involve college. Maybe they involve special training, or they could include working in the family business. Do you like to travel, or would you prefer to stay closer to home? Do you like working with people? Words? Numbers? The answers to these questions become the different areas of your mental goals garden. The quiz at the end of this chapter will help you plan your mental garden for your future.

Thinking about goals brings the results of those thoughts. When you plan for the success of your garden, consider the three kinds of goals:

immediate, short term, and long term. In a real garden, an immediate goal would be to plant enough vegetable seeds for a salad. The short term goal might be to harvest those vegetables when they ripen. A long term goal could be to plant enough vegetables to sell, thereby covering your gardening expenses. In your mental garden, consider your three kinds of goals. What do you want today? Next week? Next month? Next year? In five years? When you know the answers to those questions, you can begin to focus your thoughts on the big picture. Only then can you reap the rewards of your focused thoughts on your goals.

After you have your plan for a garden, you need the seeds. What are the seeds of a mental garden? They are all the many ways that you will achieve your goals. For example, if you have a mental garden plot labeled "Driver's License," the seeds in that garden would be your driver's manual, behind-the-wheel instruction, and a year of experience. Do you see the three goals in that scenario? The immediate goal is to get your permit by studying the driver's manual. The short term goal is to learn how to drive on the road. The long term goal is to eventually get your permanent license after the year of experience. That's how the seeds of thought work. Do you remember the Wishes vs. Thoughts in the introduction of this book? There were no wishes at all there. Instead, they were simply strong, focused, positive thoughts planted as seeds in your mental garden that led to the realization of your goal.

Now let's look at the weeds in your mental garden. Let's say you've planned for a beautiful flower garden rich in color, scent, and visual appeal. You planted the seeds. But, then you left it alone and went on to something else. The thoughts that you planted as seeds will wither and die without constant tending. You need to water, fertilize, and weed your mental garden. How? With constant attention to detail and outcomes, and the elimination of distractions.

Watch out for the pests... the rodents, the aphids, and the blight that infect and destroy your wonderful mental garden. You know them. They're the people who try to replace your thoughts with theirs, eat away at your self-esteem, and distract you from your goals. If you have a strong mental garden where you pay constant attention to detail, outcomes, and distractions, those pests won't be able to attack your mental harvest – the realization of your goals.

Remember, you reap what you sow. If you plant daisy seeds, you get daisies. If you plant weeds, you get weeds. If you plant the seeds of satisfaction in your mental garden, you will be satisfied with your efforts. However, if you plant the seeds of revenge, you'll get revenge, which is an ugly weed in anyone's garden.

You've planned, planted, tended, and harvested your mental garden. Perhaps you now have your driver's license, a job you enjoy, or a new relationship with someone special. It's time to sit back and appreciate the results of your efforts.

With appreciation, all of your physical and mental hard work can bring even more pleasure. Give yourself a small reward for a job well done. In other words, take time to smell the roses! When you do that, the next mental garden becomes easier to maintain.

Take this interest survey to help you plan for your goals.
Answer the following five questions, but feel free to add your own answer if you feel none of the answers apply to you.

1. Which do you prefer to do on a Saturday afternoon?
    a. Play sports
    b. Listen to music
    c. Play video games
    d. Read
    e. Talk with friends
    f. Shop
    g. Other _____

2.   Which of these is your favorite subject?
   a.   Science
   b.   Math
   c.   English
   d.   History
   e.   Foreign language
   f.   Other _____

3.   Which of these would you choose for an extra subject?
   a.   Art
   b.   Music
   c.   Wood or metal shop
   d.   Home arts
   e.   Computers
   f.   Other _____

4.   What did you enjoy most when you were little?
   a.   Playing board games
   b.   Playing video games
   c.   Playing outside
   d.   Creating things
   e.   Fixing things
   f.   Reading books
   g.   Other _____

5.   If you had to show your life in a creative way, which would you choose?
   a.   Journal in a diary
   b.   Draw a picture
   c.   Develop a game
   d.   Sing a song
   e.   Create a PowerPoint presentation
   f.   Other _____

Now that you have a better idea of what you consider fun, how do those answers relate to your goals? Only you have the answer to that question! Use the answers above to create enjoyable goals and rewards. Thoughtful and concrete goals, when paired with an appreciation of good work, create a healthy mental garden. These are the next beads in your beaded chain!

Goals

Pick any topic. What are your immediate goals? Your short term goals? Your long term goals?

Appreciation

How will you celebrate your achievements? What will you do to remind yourself that your work was worthwhile?

Now draw your mental garden. Divide it into four sections that indicate immediate, short-term, and long-term goals. The fourth section will contain your plans for appreciation. Your sections do not all have to be the same size, nor do they all have to be rectangles! Look at the big picture – do you see a pattern? How does that pattern relate to your goals?

"What you get by achieving your goals is not as important as what you become by achieving your goals."

~ Henry David Thoreau, American poet, author, and philosopher

who wrote Walden, a reflection on living a simple life.

CHAPTER THREE – THE MOAT
Security

What is the purpose of a castle's moat? To keep out invaders and other unwanted guests, of course! What is the purpose of a mental moat? To keep out invaders from your thoughts and unwanted guests from influencing your thoughts.

You can actually protect yourself from both physical and emotional danger with your thoughts. Remember poor Melanie who worried that she would fail the chemistry test, and then that's exactly what she did? Worrying about having a car accident or fear of falling down the stairs has the same effect. When you think about something in a negative manner, those negative thoughts collect into a magnetic force that causes accidents to happen. Your brain translates that concentrated thought on the problem and says, "Well, if that's what you want, that's what you'll get." Focus on what you want, rather than what you don't want in your mental kingdom. A mental moat can come in very handy for this.

Here is how a mental moat works. Consider your average medieval moat. The wider the moat, the more protection the residents had from invaders. The more dangerous alligators they put in their moat, the less likely invaders would be to cross. You may consider a computer firewall to be a kind of technical moat, keeping undesirable viruses and worms from your laptop.

Your mental moat needs many shields and defense mechanisms to guard against mental invaders. You're probably not like Bella in *Breaking Dawn* with the ability to put up a mental shield any time you want, but the concept is similar. Mental barriers prevent other people from influencing your thoughts, thereby influencing your behavior.

Mental shields can take the form of saying a vehement, "No," when you think something is wrong. That is the ultimate thought/action connection. A mental shield could mean that you ignore the negative comments someone says about you or a friend. That involves even more self control, more mental strength, than simply saying no. Your mental moat needs to be wide and dangerous to other people trying to invade your mental kingdom with their thoughts.

Your mental moat must be strong enough to deflect attacks on your thoughts. Picture your thoughts behind your castle walls, way beyond the moat that protects them. There, they are yours. Nobody can touch your deepest thoughts. If your moat is wide enough and your mental shield strong enough, you have the ultimate control over your thoughts. That control over your thoughts will eventually display itself as control over your actions and the way your life plays out. Isn't that exactly what you want?

Some of you may use verbal weapons, but that's not what a mental moat is all about. Fashion your weapons using thoughts instead of spoken words. Sure, you may occasionally have a direct link from your brain to your mouth, but the mental moat eliminates that, too. With the mental moat, your verbal exit from your mental castle is just as difficult as allowing invaders into your kingdom.

What are examples of thought weapons? Every time you say to yourself, "Let it go," or "I don't care what she says about me," you use your mental weapons to translate into actions. You don't actually have to say those words; you simply have to think them. That's the beauty of using your thoughts to control your actions. Words never need to get in the way.

Your mental moat is your best defense mechanism to prevent you from doing or saying something you'll regret later. It is your personal shield that prevents other people from controlling your personal thoughts. And those are your next two beads for your beaded chain: defense mechanisms and a personal shield.

What positive thoughts can you tell yourself during a personal attack? What other defense mechanisms do you have in your mental moat?_____

_____

_____

How effective is your personal shield? How can you bounce other people's thoughts back at them without hurting them in the process?_____

_____

_____

_____

Draw a picture of your personal moat. Include the defense mechanisms floating in it. What about your personal shield? What does it look like?

CHAPTER FOUR – THE SPA
Serenity

Every kingdom has a spa where the residents go to relax and rejuvenate themselves. It is a place with soft music, natural spring water, and relaxed comfort. A trip to the spa helps busy people get away from the madness of their everyday lives to rejoice in the person they are. The healing effects of spas go back thousands of years to ancient societies where the people also knew the value of relaxation.

In your mental kingdom, you don't need to spend hundreds of dollars for a private spa treatment complete with massage, aromatherapy, and a sauna. All you need is a quiet place where you can enter your mental kingdom for a while to explore its inner realms.

Relaxation will allow productive thoughts to enter your mental kingdom. However, before you relax your mind, you must first relax your body. Follow these simple directions, and then let your mind wander through your mental kingdom.

1. Find a quiet, private place. This may be difficult if you come from a busy house or a large family. It may require some creative planning, but it will be worth the effort.

2. Optional: Put on soft, relaxing music. If this bothers you, don't put on any music at all.

3. Also optional: If you enjoy fragrances, use a lavender scent. Lavender has been proven to increase relaxation. However, don't use a real candle; use a battery-powered candle or similar object. If you fall asleep during this exercise, a lit candle burning unattended could be very dangerous. Natural lemon scents are also effective anti-anxiety agents.

4. Either lie down or recline in an easy chair with your feet up.

5. Dim the lights and close your eyes.

6. Think about relaxing every part of your body, beginning with your toes and ending with your head. Take one body part at a time and concentrate on relaxing that part. When you are convinced that each part is as relaxed as possible, move on.

7. When you are completely relaxed, let your mind wander through your mental kingdom with no goal at all. Don't think about problems, goals, or what you'll do after your mental spa treatment. The idea is to do absolutely nothing mentally for a while to rejuvenate your brain. Sometimes it's good to think about nothing at all!

8. You may fall asleep, and that's fine! When you awaken, you'll feel mentally awake and aware and better able to tackle life's difficulties.

Why is the mental spa experience so vital to the health of your mental kingdom? Because your achievements grow as seeds in your subconscious. When you relax your conscious mind, you allow your subconscious mind to take over. During that aimless rambling through your mental kingdom spa treatment, you may find answers to questions you never thought to ask. You may find an idea you never considered. The subconscious mind is a powerful tool in helping the conscious mind to structure its thoughts. If the subconscious mind lays buried beneath layers of dust from the activity of the conscious mind, you'll never know what messages it carries for you. You can organize your thoughts, plant the seeds of ideas, and tend your mental garden. But without the assistance of your subconscious mind, you simply touch the surface of your mind's capability to achieve your goals.

The thoughts of your subconscious mind are the glue that holds the conscious thoughts together, whether you are aware of it or not. The subconscious mind actually controls more of your actions than your conscious mind. That's why it is so important to allow your subconscious mind to come out and play once in a while.

How often should you get in touch with your subconscious mind by going to your mental spa? Several times a week is ideal, but if you have time for only once a week, that's better than once a month or never getting in touch with your subconscious mind. With that in mind, please add the next two beads for your beaded chain: relaxation and meditation.

Relaxation When and where do you feel most relaxed? What do you see around the room in your mental spa?_____

_____

_____

_____

_____

Meditation How can you help your mind wander while you relax in your mental spa? _____

_____

_____

_____

_____

_____

_____

Draw an abstract picture of your mind wandering around your mental spa.

CHAPTER FIVE – THE PHARMACY
Wellness

When you go into your local pharmacy, you find everything from candy to toys to beauty products to medicine. It is a mini-mall under one roof. The original pharmacies dispensed advice as often as they sold pills and **elixirs** for specific ills. What is in your mental pharmacy? Healthy thoughts, naturally!

Natural remedies allow the mind to settle into a routine, so you can consider your problems clearly. Healthy minds do not easily become addicted to substances, objects, or people. Remember – thoughts are magnetic. Healthy thoughts pull healthy thoughts with them. Unhealthy thoughts are also just as magnetic, but not nearly as good for you.

Healthy thoughts sit on the mental pharmacy shelf until you need them. They carry labels like creativity, imagination, faith, acceptance, charity, love, forgiveness, enthusiasm, friendship, responsibility, courage, hope, empathy, diligence, trust, optimism, and any other positive trait you can think of. They all sit on the shelf, waiting for the day when your mental kingdom needs them to cope with the circumstances of your life.

Pay attention to the person behind the counter. The mental pharmacist decides which package you need for unique situations. For example, suppose you found out that your uncle just went into the hospital. Your friendly mental pharmacist would recommend that you take a dose of empathy and hope to deal with your feelings as you enter your uncle's hospital room. Or maybe your entire family is going to the mountains for vacation, but you prefer the beach. In that case, your friendly mental pharmacist would recommend Acceptance and Enthusiasm. With so much acceptance and enthusiasm in your mental kingdom, your thoughts would have a hard time turning to sulkiness and rejection during your trip.

One of the strongest elixirs in your mental pharmacy is labeled **philanthropy**. When you help other people, you are engaging in philanthropy. That's different from charity, which means you give something away like money, old clothes, or cans for the food drive. Philanthropy involves actively doing something to improve other people's lives. Philanthropy forces you to think in a positive manner about how you can do some good in this world. You might consider volunteering at a nursing home, helping out at an animal rescue facility, or reading to children in the library. When you take the elixir of philanthropy off your mental shelf, you begin to force your thoughts away from yourself and toward others.

Philanthropy is a powerful **catharsis** for your mind. It allows you to atone for the times when you might not have been as kind as you should have been to someone else. Philanthropy gives you that feel-good, warm-all-over-feeling that encourages thoughts to be as healthy as possible. When you help others, you are actually helping yourself at the same time.

The mental pharmacy is the place in your kingdom where you go for mental help dealing with your everyday problems. Have you guessed the next two beads on your beaded chain? They are health and philanthropy.

Can you think of any other healthy labels you can put on the bottles of your mental pharmacy? What happens when you combine several of those bottles? _____

_____

_____

_____

What would you like to change? How can you change that need into thoughts that will control your actions into doing some kind of philanthropy? _____

_____

_____

_____

Draw a picture of your mental pharmacy with the labels on all the packages.

"Although we are all the same in not wanting problems and wanting a peaceful life, we tend to create a lot of problems for ourselves. Encountering those problems, anger develops and overwhelms our mind, which leads to violence. A good way to counter this and to work for a more peaceful world is to develop concern for others. Then our anger, jealousy and other destructive emotions will naturally weaken and diminish."

~ Dalai Lama, Tibetan spiritual leader

CHAPTER SIX – THE MARKET
Choices

verybody loves choices. Which movie should I watch? Which cereal can I have for breakfast? What should I get my friend for his birthday? When you make a choice, you consciously think about your preferences. You focus your thoughts momentarily on whether you want a juicy hamburger or the healthier veggie burger. In your mental kingdom, you have warehouses of choices. All you have to do is make the right decision about what to take with you from those warehouses. When you have positive thoughts operating to your advantage, your conscious and subconscious minds work together to help you make good choices.

As in any market, the items on the shelves present you with wise choices and poor choices. Let's examine the cereal aisle where there are a hundred different cereal boxes. You've probably been told over and over that sugary cereals are bad choices and whole grain cereals are good choices. But those sugary cereals sure taste better! Do you see what just happened? Somebody else got into your mental kingdom and told you to eat the sugary cereal rather than the whole grain one. That person is probably that guy on TV advertising Sweet Flakes!

Now let's look into the market of your mental kingdom. You have the same sugary vs. whole grain choices, only you may want to think of them a bit more generally, perhaps as "help vs. hindrance." You have the independence to make good decisions now that you're a member of *The Beaded Kingdom*, right? And you have set some positive goals for yourself. So, now look at the sugary vs. whole grain cereals again. Nobody tells you which one to eat, but because you are an independent thinker, the magnetic thoughts in your mental kingdom pull together to say, "The sugary cereal tastes sweeter, but the whole grain cereal is healthier and will help me reach my goal of losing ten pounds easier." See the linking? Your thoughts influenced your actions. Nobody told you what to do because you figured it out all by yourself. In other words, you offered yourself the choice of sugar vs. whole grains and made the best decision based on your goals. Wow!

While we're in the market, let's talk about nutrition. You can't have healthy thoughts without a healthy brain. Your brain uses 20% of your daily calorie intake. So, if the average person eats 1600 calories per day, your brain needs 320 calories to do its job. I'm going to get a little technical here and tell you that the frontal lobe of your brain is where you do your thinking. It is particularly sensitive to insufficient glucose levels. Other areas of the brain that control movement and sensory impressions are a bit hardier. When your glucose level drops, it's the frontal cortex that suffers. Your thinking becomes clouded, although you may retain the ability to listen to music and maintain your heart rate. A healthy brain needs proper nutrition to think clearly.

You may be wondering, since the word glucose means sugar, why the sugary cereals aren't actually good for you. Unfortunately, you digest sugars very quickly. They give you a rush of energy followed by a sluggish slowdown. So, the sugary cereal you ate a 6:00 am gave you enough energy to get dressed, hop on the bus, and make it to homeroom on time. However, it didn't give you enough energy to get through your first three classes without falling asleep.

That's why the whole grain cereal was a better choice. Your body digests whole grains more slowly, so you have energy and glucose in your brain for a longer period of time. Indeed, the key to a healthy brain is a balanced diet. So, even if you chose a whole grain cereal, eating it all day long would rob your brain of other important nutrients, such a protein. Look on the shelves of your real supermarket. There you'll find a variety of healthy and not-so-healthy food choices. Below is a partial list of the scientifically proven best and the worst foods for thought processing.

Write each food in the column that describes its effect on the brain.

Salmon, Walnuts, Sugary Foods, Kiwi Fruit, Caffeine, Whole Grains, Syrups, Plain Pancakes, White Chocolate, Butter, Chips, Blueberries, Low-Fat Yogurt, Avocados, Milk, Frosting, Alcohol, Plain Bagels, Low-Fat Peanut Butter, Brown Rice, Nicotine, Fruit, Vegetables, Peppermint Tea, Ice Cream, Cake, Soy, Chicken Caesar Salad, Spinach Salad, Doughnuts, Turkey, Decaffeinated Coffee

BRAIN
BOOSTERS

BRAIN
BUSTERS

Brain Boosters: Salmon, Walnuts, Kiwi Fruit, Whole Grains, Blueberries, Low-Fat Yogurt, Avocados, Milk, Low-Fat Peanut Butter, Brown Rice, Fruit, Vegetables, Peppermint Tea, Soy, Chicken Caesar Salad, Spinach, Turkey, Decaffeinated Coffee
Brain Busters: Sugary Foods, Caffeine, Syrups, Plain Pancakes, White Chocolate, Butter, Chips, Frosting, Alcohol, Ice Cream, Cake, Doughnuts

34

So, what choices do you see in your mental market now that you understand how to have a healthy brain?   Here are the next two beads in your Beaded chain: choices and nutrition.

Think about a time when you had very little choice in a decision. How can you use your mental mansion to twist your thoughts so that you do have choices in a decision?_____

_____

_____

_____

_____

How will you make your brain healthier now that you know that certain foods are better for your brain? Develop a sample daily diet that includes nutritious food. _____

_____

_____

_____

_____

Go into your mental market and look on the shelves. Draw what you see there. Label all the packages by their good choices, such as getting enough sleep, eating the right food, etc.

"In the long run, we shape our lives, and we shape ourselves. The process never ends until we die. And the choices we make are ultimately our own responsibility."

~ Eleanor Roosevelt

CHAPTER SEVEN – THE WORKSHOP
Creativity

t's hard to make good choices without the creativity to consider your alternatives. Sometimes you don't see your alternatives because your jumbled thoughts control your creativity. Creative thought allows you to broaden your ideas and your ideals. Creative thought allows you to see every aspect of a situation. Creative thought, when focused, will help you to achieve your goals because it will influence your actions.

Remember the fun you had in art class? Or wood shop? Or metal shop? Or any other hands-on activity that allowed you to be creative? Why was it so much fun? Because you could use the materials in the room to develop your own creation. There were no wrong answers. What you created was yours because you decided how you wanted your creation to look.

But maybe your weren't that satisfied with your creation. Perhaps you tried to make it look just like a model, and you became dissatisfied with the results. Why? Because you allowed someone else's creativity (the creator of the model) to influence your ability to develop your own unique picture, or sculpture, or wooden device. In this chapter, we're going to delve into the workshop of your mental kingdom to find tools for thought that you can use to reach your goals. When you use your imagination to consider all your choices, you make better decisions.

Do You Have a Big But?

Yes, I spelled that last word correctly! When you add *but* to the end of any statement, you add an element of creativity to your thinking. Finish these sentences using positive thinking to control your life. Afterward, explain how positive thoughts will translate into positive actions.

*Last week, I forgot to take out the trash, but*_____

_____ *so* _____

_____

*I like to wear new clothes, but*_____

_____ *so* _____

_____

I want to make the team, but _____

_____ *so* _____

_____

Need more help? Here are some possible answers:

Last week, I forgot to take out the trash, but I had too much else to do, *so* this week, I'll make a big note so nobody else has to do extra work that I should have done.

I like to wear new clothes, but I don't have the money, *so* I'll be satisfied with what I have until I get more money.

I want to make the team, but my skills are just not good enough, *so* I'll find another activity that I can do well.

Do you see how the sample answers didn't include excuses? They are the result of careful thought that involved taking control over the situation by creatively thinking about the consequences. Some also involved simply accepting that you can't change the situation. Either way, your positive thoughts made you feel better about what was going on in your life.

Other ways to think creatively include considering alternatives and priorities. Imagine this crazy week: Your sister is getting married … at a **destination wedding**, you have finals, and your best friend is moving three states away. An ordinary person would become overwhelmed with just one of those events. A member of *The Beaded Kingdom* knows that his or her mental kingdom includes creative thought to produce solutions.

Here's one solution: Study early and get the finals out of the way. Then, have a send-off party for your friend before you leave for your sister's destination wedding. *The Beaded Kingdom* resident planted an end-of-the–school-year plot in her mental garden that included seeds labeled "Finals first," "Show friend you care," and "Enjoy sis's wedding." All of the above went off without a hitch, and the potentially overwhelmed beaded kingdom resident got everything done without stress.

Another aspect of your mental workshop is to trust in your creativity. You have the mental tools to fashion a great solution to your problems... if you allow yourself to trust in the outcome. A real workshop has wrenches, brushes, and other items necessary to finish a creation. Your mental workshop has a huge box of trust: trust that you are capable of creative thought, trust that your intuition is correct, and trust that you will follow through with your creative decisions. Next to that box of trust are other tools: glue to bind your thoughts together, **sieves** to separate good ideas from bad, and sandpaper to smooth the rough edges of your ideas. You can probably think of many other tools for that workshop shelf. The next two beads on your chain are imagination and trust.

Imagination Think of one thing you'd like to change in your life. Now consider three or four ways to approach a solution to that problem. Did you come up with any new ideas? _____

_____

_____

_____

Trust What are some things that you can say to convince yourself to trust your instincts and to go with your creative ideas?

_____

_____

_____

_____

_____

Draw a picture of the creative tools in your mental workshop.

CHAPTER EIGHT – THE GYM
Activity

I f you think you know what's going to be in this chapter, you're probably right. A healthy mind is an active mind, just as a healthy body is an active body. Let's get your brain working out using mental gymnastics. Too much work? Not if the exercise is fun. It's like the difference between doing sit-ups and playing basketball. They both achieve the purpose of exercising your body, but basketball is so much more fun.

In order for your mind to develop creative thoughts and plant the seeds of goals, your mind needs to get ready for these activities. Mental gymnastics require a mental fitness center for a good workout. And just like physical fitness, mental fitness should begin easy and work up to vigorous exercise. When you begin easy, you don't become as frustrated with yourself as when you jump right into mental gymnastics.

What are some easy mental gymnastics? Play a memory game with a preschooler. Do crossword puzzles labeled "easy." Solve a simple Sudoku puzzle. Think of three unusual uses for a common object. Play Scrabble with

40

a ten-year-old. Do a 200-piece jigsaw puzzle. Any easy game that requires creative thinking qualifies as easy mental gymnastics.

After you find a fun mental activity that you enjoy and want to repeat, then start building endurance, the same way an athlete trains her body. Play games against more advanced players, solve more complex Sudoku puzzles, think of ten things to do with that common object, and leave the "easy" jigsaw puzzles for less advanced mental gymnasts.

You can also try learning something new. If you don't know anything about how to fix a car, take auto shop as your elective class. Or read a book on how the pyramids were built. Create a poem or a rap about a baseball, a lampshade, or a tulip. Complete at least one mental activity each day so your mental gym in your mental kingdom doesn't have time to get dusty and rusty.

Mental exercise isn't the only workout you need to have a healthy brain. Physical exercise also helps your brain stay strong and more able to generate positive creative thoughts. Your brain demands oxygen to do its job well, and you need physical exercise to get that oxygen to your brain.

Couch potatoes have three problems. First, they don't actively use their brains while they watch TV. Second, they don't move their bodies around to get oxygen to their brains. Third, while they sit there not thinking and not moving, they're probably eating all the wrong foods. Nothing is worse for a healthy brain and your mental kingdom than being a couch potato.

Walking quite literally clears your head. It increases oxygen to your brain because the exercise moves your blood around faster. Exercise also releases those happy endorphins that help you feel better about yourself. Think about all the opportunities you have to get more exercise for brain health. Waiting for your popcorn in the microwave? Do some running in place for those three minutes. Going to the mall? Walk briskly around, then stroll the stores. Were you sitting all day in school? Then when you get home, do something active like riding your bike, dancing, or shooting some hoops. Continuously think about ways to move more oxygen into your brain.

A strong healthy brain involves mental gymnastics and physical exercise. Here are two new beads for your beaded chain: active thoughts and physical exercise.

Active Thoughts What types of mental gymnastics do you enjoy? What new things might you learn to strain your brain? _____

_____

_____

_____

_____

Physical Exercise List three new ways to incorporate exercise into your everyday routine. _____

_____

_____

_____

_____

Draw a picture that includes exercise equipment in the gym of your mental kingdom.

CHAPTER NINE – THE PEOPLE
Relationships

ook around your mental kingdom. You now notice the buildings and gardens, but you should also see thousands of people going about their everyday business. Each person has a different life, a different agenda, and different relationships. They also all have the potential to sidetrack you from your positive thoughts. Each time you meet someone, touch your beaded chain to remind yourself that you have ultimate control over your thoughts and actions.

Do you believe everything you hear on TV? Of course not! Some news reports may be wrong. Some advertisements lead you to believe that their product is the best possible thing for you. Then why do you believe everything other people say about you, especially when you learn that it was said behind your back? You believe these things because you allowed yourself to believe them. You allowed your mental workers to lower the drawbridge and let those negative thoughts into your kingdom. To be a positive thinker, you would do well to avoid this people trap and, instead, give yourself permission to make your own decisions about the things that concern you.

Let's go back to Melanie and Mario. The people in Melanie's life probably tell her she's a klutz. She always runs into things, knocks things over, and falls down. Of course she does! That's because she believes the people who call her a klutz. How did that happen? Perhaps many years ago, Melanie had a bad moment and tripped over a cord, knocked down a lamp, and then banged her head on the wall. Unfortunately, someone witnessed this and called her a klutz, or worse, "Mishap Melanie." The name stuck because she allowed herself to believe the person who called her "Mishap Melanie."

Mario, on the other hand, had several good days in a row many years ago. He aced his math test, earned a seat at the state spelling bee, and won first place in the science fair. Mario rejoiced in all the good thoughts coming his way. People at school began calling him "Mighty Mario" because he could do no wrong. And those thoughts escalated. Each time he set a new goal, Mario seemed to come out on top. Eventually, the little voice inside his mental kingdom began to tell Mario the same things that other people were saying about him. If they would have called him a loser, then that little voice probably would have echoed that thought over and over again instead. However, they told him he was awesome and, even after all this time, Mario still believes.

So, how can you block the bad echoes and encourage the good echoes? Go back to the market in your mental kingdom and select an imaginary mirror. Put that up outside of your castle so that all the bad echoes reflect back to the person who sent the message that you're a loser. Put up a mental sign that only good messages are allowed across the drawbridge. That way, you think of only your positive traits, which will eventually overshadow your negative traits. It's really a very easy process to pull out of a bad self-impression. Any time somebody tries to invade your mental kingdom, touch your beaded chain and remember that you have ultimate control over your thoughts.

Now there is one more way that you can eliminate negative thoughts when you interact with other people. Warning: I'm going to get a little preachy here and tell you what not to do because you may not even realize that you're doing it: don't define who you are by who you hang around with. In other words, be yourself. When you define yourself by your friends, you're telling yourself that you must be like them in order to be a whole person. Nothing could be further from the truth! When you say that you "belong" to your boyfriend or girlfriend, a little part of you disappears and reforms in the other person's head. Ouch! That must hurt! Make sure you are strong enough to stand on your own, and you will have much healthier relationships.

Like the song goes, are you "looking for love in all the wrong places?" This is an easy answer. Love yourself first, and the rest of your relationships will fall into place around you. Insecure people tend to attract insecure people. Is that what you want? Of course not! Be strong in your **convictions**, and you will attract people who will help to maintain the walls of your mental kingdom, rather than tear them down. When others tear down your walls, you are the only one who can put them back up again, and that is much more work than simply attracting people in the first place who will help to maintain them in good working order.

What about support groups? People who share the same problems or personalities can be a huge influence - sometimes positively, but sometimes negatively. A professionally-guided support group can be quite valuable. They help you to see that you're not alone in this world with your thoughts and feelings. However, an impromptu support group of friends may not give you the best advice. Support groups are like mental trampolines. The professional support groups have a net around them to catch you if you go off the side. A support group of friends is simply a bunch of people jumping around without the net. You might end up getting hurt more by listening to their advice, so be careful!

Finally, there are two more types of people in your mental kingdom that should have a huge *Caution!* sign over their heads. These people are the Jealous Johns and the Control Freak Frannies. If you have friends who are jealous of your actions or of the people you spend time with (or friends who try to control your life in any way), then they are not really your friends. Avoid these mental magnets because they will pull all the energy from your mental kingdom. True friends are the people who respect who you are and allow you to think independently.

Have you guessed yet what your next two beads are?

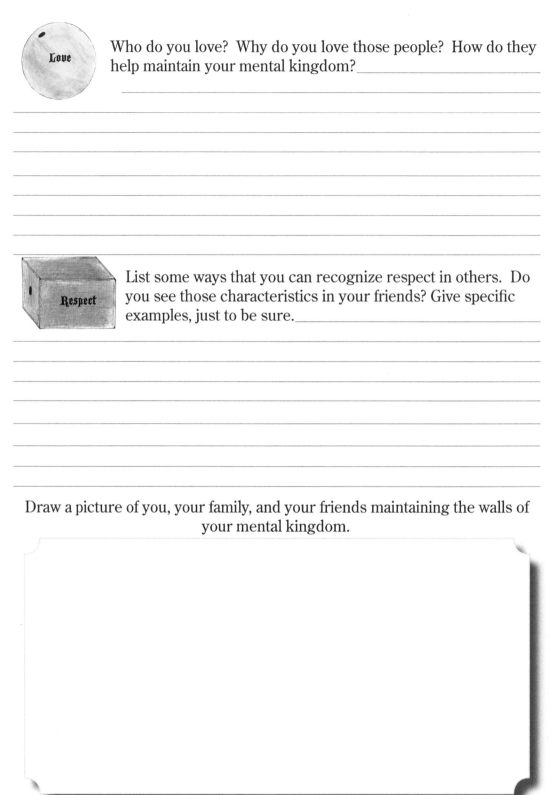

Love Who do you love? Why do you love those people? How do they help maintain your mental kingdom?_____

_____

_____

_____

_____

_____

_____

_____

Respect List some ways that you can recognize respect in others. Do you see those characteristics in your friends? Give specific examples, just to be sure._____

_____

_____

_____

_____

_____

_____

_____

Draw a picture of you, your family, and your friends maintaining the walls of your mental kingdom.

CHAPTER TEN – THE WEATHER
Change

ook outside your window – your real window. What do you see? Perhaps rain, snow, wind, or a bright sunny day. What did you see yesterday? Probably something different, right? The same is true of your mental kingdom. Every day is different. The way you react to that change depends on your strength to adapt. How you think about change will also influence your actions during life's transitions.

Change always involves a learning curve. The first time something new happens, you must adjust to new circumstances. The second time it happens, you know how you reacted the first time. You'll either repeat a successful response or change because it didn't go so well the first time. Change is inevitable, but how you deal with change depends on how strongly you can cope with that change.

Think about all the changes, both tiny and huge, in your life. You change class from math to science – that's a tiny change. You move two streets over, but stay in the same school district – that's a bigger change. Your parents get divorced, and you move five states away with Mom and Grandma – that's a huge change. You accept the tiny changes without question and simply go with the flow. You may be flexible enough to realize that your parents want a different-sized house for some reason, so again you go with the flow. However, during a divorce, you may get angry, belligerent, and negative. You might feel like the whole thing is all your fault (which it certainly isn't!), or you may become moody and depressed. None of these reactions indicates a strong mental kingdom, able to accept whatever weather comes along. Flexibility is the key to acceptance.

How you think about change influences how you deal with it. So board up your mental windows, get lots of canned goods in your cabinets, and get ready for the mental hurricane that occurs during extreme change.

Most change comes with warning signals. Sometimes you are totally unaware of those signals until the change hits your life like a derailed freight train. Suddenly your life is all messed up, and you don't know how to start cleaning it up. So you walk away, but the mess is still there taunting you to do something, anything, to clean it up. Let's look at some warning signals that can help you to cope with major changes, preventing them from running you down like that freight train.

Look around you. What do you see? Do you see a two-bedroom house, parents with a decent income, and three younger brothers? Those are your warning signs that your parents may be planning to buy a new house. Do you hear your parents arguing all the time? Does one parent leave frequently? Those are your signals that a divorce may be coming. When you mentally prepare for change, the freight train goes off on a different track and doesn't derail. It may take a while to get it back on the right track again, but it will eventually reach its destination intact.

The storms in your mental kingdom are like the actual storms outside your window; they come and they go, but they don't last forever. Sometimes they leave a mess to clean up, but sometimes they give way to sunnier weather. Let's see how you can prepare to deal with the inevitable changes in your life like a move, a breakup with a boyfriend or girlfriend, or a new baby in the family. The ability to deal with change happens gradually, with practice and flexibility.

There are a million ways you can practice dealing with change – here are a few:

☐ Move the furniture in your room.

☐ Decorate a plain notebook.

☐ Walk a different way to your next class (as long as it gets you there on time!).

☐ Put your left sock on first (most people put their right sock on first!).

☐ Try writing with your non-dominant hand occasionally, perhaps while doodling.

☐ Get outside of your comfort zone by trying a new sport, reading a new book genre, listening to a different type of music, or watching an **obscure** TV program.

Learning to cope with changes is the same as learning any new thing; practice makes perfect. Although you may not immediately notice the connection, regularly dealing with small changes (like the ones above) will help you to deal with life's bigger changes as they come along. But you must always keep in mind that you simply cannot change some things. In these occasions, your only healthy choice is to accept the change, and move on with your life. I know that's easier said than done, but with the help of tools from your strong mental kingdom, you can adjust more easily, especially if you've been practicing on small changes.

When a large change comes, go to your mental kingdom garden, and look at all the good things in your life that will not change. Schedule a mental kingdom spa day to relax and separate yourself from thoughts about the change. Go to your mental kingdom gym, and do some mental gymnastics. When you adjust your thinking about change, you will also change your actions and general outlook on life.

Look forward, not backward. If you are changing your school, changing your house, or changing the people who live with you, consider the advantages. Instead of looking backward and saying, "I'll never see my friends again," look forward and say, "I wonder what kind of new friends I'll make." See how that works? Look forward to the advantages and possibilities in your new situation. Then, when the storm hits, you'll be better prepared to ride it out because you'll know that the sunny days will indeed return. Your beaded chain will remind you of this critical thought.

If you've gone through your entire mental kingdom searching for emotional relief, but you're still struggling with a hurricane-sized problem, don't hesitate to get help. Go to your parents and tell them what you're thinking. If you can't go to them for some reason, then see a counselor or another family member. Nobody should have to endure life's transitions alone. Just make sure that the people you trust with your thoughts (who often bring with them their own strong thoughts and opinions) don't pull you down even further into the storm. Use the next two beads on your chain for guidance in a storm.

Flexibility Think of a time when your life changed. How were you flexible enough to see the positive aspects of that change? _____

_____

Acceptance What are some life transitions that you can't change? They may require changing your thoughts from denial to acceptance. What can you do to accept the things you can't change?

_____

_____

Draw a picture of a change in your life. Include people who helped you and the thoughts you had during that change. It's okay to show the negative thoughts, as long as you also show how you transformed them into positive thoughts about the future. (Use the **Notes** section at back of book for more space.)

"Acceptance of what has happened is the first step to overcoming the consequences of any misfortune."
~William James, American psychologist and philosopher.

CHAPTER ELEVEN – THE ANIMALS
Life Lessons

No mental kingdom is ever complete without its own animal kingdom. The people in your mental kingdom rely on animals for comfort and companionship. They also need them to learn lessons from nature. From the tiniest ant to the heaviest horse, animals can teach us nearly as much as we can learn from books, if we would take the time to observe and consider their activities.

The butterflies (Engage Life) – This lesson is easy if you think about it long enough – get out of your cocoon! Every season, butterflies begin as caterpillars and then emerge from their cocoons as colorful butterflies. They let go of the past and look to the future. They ride the wind and smell the flowers. When you stay locked in your mental cocoon, you live a solitary existence. You don't show the world how truly wonderful you can be. Be like the butterfly - allow yourself to grow wings and fly into the future!

The bees (Harmony) - Bees have a very supportive system in which every insect knows its job and performs it to the best of its ability for the good of the hive. They are so organized in their efforts that they actually plan for the future of the hive. Everything they do ensures that the hive will support future generations of bees. They are completely loyal to each other! Be like the bees - spend every waking minute doing something that will be good for your future. How awesome is that!

The birds (Be Industrious) – Can you hear them? They are Mother Nature's chorus, singing every morning to greet the new day. Their pleasant voices attract other birds to answer them. They build complex nests for their families, safe from predators, and when baby birds are born, they strive to become independent. Birds are loyal to themselves. Be like the birds - allow only positive words to come from your mouth, and help around the house to protect your "nest."

The squirrels (Persevere) – Squirrels are among the most adaptable creatures in your mental kingdom. If one branch doesn't work, they immediately scramble for another, and then another... until they find one that is just right for them. Like the bees, they also plan for the future by hiding acorns to prepare for the hardships of winter.

How can you become like a squirrel? Try different solutions to your problems. If one solution doesn't work, try another and then another... until you your problem is solved. As a squirrel, your acorns will represent the life lessons you've already learned. Collect these lessons in a journal, and reread them when times are hard. These will guide you as, like the squirrels, you adapt to unfamiliar events and plan for the future.

The fish (Positive Environment)- This lesson is easy – stay in school! Actually, fish swim in schools for safety. The adage, "there's safety in numbers" could have originated with someone observing a school of fish. If you have a hundred fish in one place, it becomes less likely that the predator will target a specific fish. Be like fish - stay in school and surround yourself with positive influences, so you become less likely to be the target of a bully.

The horses (Teamwork)– Do you see the pattern emerging? What characteristic of horse behavior is a life lesson for you? It's team-work! Look at the difference between one horse pulling a farm wagon and a team of Clydesdales pulling a commercial wagon. All the Clydesdales work together. Not one horse lets the others take his load. In your mental kingdom, visualize all of your horses working together. Then, when you get assigned to a group project, you'll be more likely to pull your share of the load. Be like horses – work hard and be a valuable part of a team.

The cats (Respect)– If you love a cat, you know that you must love the cat the way that cat wants to be loved. If she likes to be scratched behind the ears, you do that. If she prefers to simply lie on your lap, you allow that. People are no different.

Most people treat others the way they want to be treated; it's the golden rule, right? Wrong! We need to treat people they way *they* want to be treated, rather than our perception of how they want to be treated.

Think about it this way: You might enjoy playing tennis on a sunny Saturday afternoon. Your friend, who is not as athletic, might prefer to play board games. You invite her to play tennis, she refuses, you get offended, and the friendship **deteriorates**. Why? Because you asked her to do what *you* wanted to do.

Certainly the actions of a friendship shouldn't always be one-sided; it's not necessary for one friend to always give in to the other friend's ideas. But occasionally, people like to be invited to do something they personally consider fun. So, be like a cat - make your preferences known, so other people will understand what you *want* to do, rather than pressuring you to follow their lead... and next time you are together, return the favor!

The dogs (Loyalty) – Finally, we come to the faithful dogs in your mental kingdom. They love you unconditionally, feel extreme loyalty to you, are easy to train, and are you constant companions. What a wonderful personality! We would all do well to be more like our dogs – friendly, loyal, and eager learners.

Here are the next two beads on your beaded chain: diligence and loyalty.

Why is it good to work consistently toward a specific goal? How have you done this, and what were the results of your efforts?

_____
_____
_____
_____

List some of the people who deserve your loyalty, and tell why you should care for them._____

_____
_____
_____
_____

Draw a picture of yourself surrounded by the animals in your mental kingdom. Include others that were not listed in this chapter. Tell what lessons you can learn from them.

"A boy can learn a lot from a dog: obedience, loyalty, and the importance of turning around three times before lying down."
~ Robert Benchley, American humorist and newspaper columnist.

CHAPTER TWELVE – THE DUNGEON
Quarantine

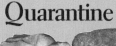 veryone has a few negative personality traits. You might occasionally feel jealous, angry, aggressive, bossy, greedy, grumpy, pessimistic, impulsive, or even **vulgar**. It's okay to feel that way as long as you don't allow those negative feelings to surface and turn into words or actions. Thoughts of success will naturally drive thoughts of failure into your mental dungeon.

Consider the medieval dungeon. That was where thieves, murderers, and other criminals were locked away to protect the rest of the people. Dungeons were dirty, infested places with heavy doors and enormous locks to prevent escapes. Now consider the dungeon in your mental kingdom. Imagine the filth and grime and vermin crawling around inside. You don't want to go there, do you? That's why it's the perfect place for all your negative personality traits! Thinking ugly thoughts? Toss them down there with the scum, and go ahead and add a negative-trait-eating dragon, for good measure. This will allow your good judgment to take over, optimism will return, and your personality will improve. Let's look at some specific negative personality traits and learn why they should meet their **demise** in your mental dungeon.

Arrogance – This is the trait that makes you feel that you are better than everyone else on the team… and you show it through your words and actions. Arrogant people constantly put others down to make themselves feel even better. If you truly do have better skills at an activity, then use that ability to help train others, rather than to belittle them. Arrogance belongs in the mental dungeon.

Profanity – People who use bad language generally don't know anything positive to say as an alternative. They curse, swear, and use vulgar language that their parents and teachers **abhor**. Or perhaps even their parents and older siblings use these objectionable words and phrases. Maybe they think that using profane words is a sign of maturity. Nothing could be further from the truth – those words are a sign of immaturity! When you are tempted to say those words, force yourself to think of alternatives. Profanity has a perfect home in the mental dungeon.

Rudeness – Most people don't even realize they are being rude, since rudeness is simply a disrespect for the **norms** of social situations. A great rule of thumb to avoid rudeness is to use the following three words or phrases generously in any social situation: "please," "thank you," and "excuse me."

When it comes to good manners, have you noticed that people often tell you what you're *not* supposed to do. *Don't* reach across the table. *Don't* rush to be first all the time. *Don't* call other people names. There are a lot of negative rules, aren't they? This is because rudeness is negative. Rudeness is all about what you're not doing, rather than what you should be doing.

Unfortunately, there aren't always specific rules to follow when it comes to rudeness, so the best thing to do around others if you are uncertain is to watch their reactions to your behavior. If you are paying attention, it should be easy to tell if you are being rude, since rude people are annoying to polite people. It's not hard to notice that someone is annoyed. Look for eye rolling, heavy sighs, arms crossed in front, angry scowls, and an attempt to avoid you. These could all be signs that you are being rude and should apologize quickly before you are mentally labeled by them as a bad friend.

Dishonesty

Dishonesty – Everybody lies. Some people lie much more than others. Others lie only to protect someone else. However, dishonesty and lying belong in the mental dungeon because they allow you to be a false person. Also, most liars don't realize this, but even though they may not act like they are on to your tricks, most people realize that they are being lied to. Don't believe me? Think back to a time when someone lied to you. How did you know they were lying? Human instincts, when it comes to lying, can be very sophisticated. And, usually, after using these instincts to discover the lie, these same humans then use these same instincts to decide whether the liar is still valuable to them as a friend. How embarrassing!

Dishonesty takes many forms: lying about your age, cheating on a test, holding back part of the truth, sneaking out of the house, and cheating on your boyfriend or girlfriend. Remember the boy who cried wolf all the time; when the wolf really appeared, nobody paid any attention to him? That's what really happens to dishonest people. When they finally decide to be honest, nobody believes them. When you put dishonesty down into your mental dungeon, you will remember to tell the truth, even if you think it may get you into trouble. In the long run, the truth will only strengthen your mental kingdom.

Pessimism

Pessimism – "This will never work." "I can't do this." "I'm not good enough to make the team." Those are all examples of pessimistic thinking. The pessimist sees the flaws in the world; the optimist sees the opportunities. The pessimist expects things to go wrong; the optimist expects them to turn out right. Basically, if you expect bad things to happen, they will; if you expect good things to happen, they will. Remember Melanie and Mario? Melanie was the pessimist. She expected to fail her test, and she did! Mario was the optimist. He expected to pass his test, and he did! So, let's turn those first sentences around to the optimistic viewpoint: "I'll figure out a way." "I can do this." "I need to practice more." Put that pessimism in your mental dungeon, lock the door, and throw away the key! You'll be much happier.

Negativity

Here are two more beads for your beaded chain.

Optimism

Think about something you want or need to do. What are some optimistic things you can say to yourself that will help you to achieve your goal? _____

_____

_____

_____

_____

_____

_____

_____

Judgment

Good judgment will allow you to put the negative personality traits in the mental dungeon and keep the good traits within your mental kingdom. Make a list of the negative traits you will put into that dungeon. _____

_____

_____

_____

_____

_____

_____

I'm going to fail.

I'll worry about it tomorrow.

I don't care if I pass.

I would rather hang with friends.

I did my best.

I'm prepared.

I got this!

I'm focused on my goal.

It will be worth the sacrifice.

Draw a picture of your castle and the dungeon. Put your positive traits in the castle's courtyard under the bright sun. Put your negative traits in the dungeon, locked behind a heavy door.

"One of the things I learned the hard way was that it doesn't pay to get discouraged. Keeping busy and making optimism a way of life can restore your faith in yourself."
~ Lucille Ball, American actress.

CONCLUSION
Your Own Room

eep inside your sparkling mental kingdom, you'll find your personal space. That's where you can do what you want, when you want. However, that space needs to be kept neat so you can find all of your positive qualities there. You know how easy it is to find something when your room is organized, right? Now think about how difficult it is to find the other shoe when you are running late and your room is a mess. Not a pretty sight, is it?

In your own personal space, you can create whatever beads you want for your beaded chain. What other qualities would you like to emphasize or improve? Give yourself some time to consider the answer to that question, and then create as many extra beads as you can. Record them below so you remember why you created them.

Maintenance of the Beaded Chain

Just as your kingdom, your castle, and your room should be maintained, so should your beaded chain. Remember to clean it occasionally. Polish the metal if it is silver, and wipe it with a clean cloth. When you touch the beads, your natural skin oils will give it a lustrous sheen, especially if your beads are wooden.

Your beaded chain links all of your positive thoughts. That is the message of this book: change your thoughts, to change your actions, to change your life. Your life may not actually change when you move away, but your attitude toward your current life will change. And that change in attitude will make all the difference in the world in making you a happier, healthier person.

So what are you waiting for? Check out the appendix and start making or buying your own special beaded chain. The very last bead you will need to complete your chain is gratitude.

Think of all the good things in your life. In the journal below, write what you would tell someone for helping to provide those good things.

Draw a picture of all those wonderful things. Draw your beaded chain in this picture, as well.

Appendix
Where to buy Beaded Chains

It's okay to buy your beaded chain if you don't have the time, skill, or desire to make one. However, make sure that your beaded chain comes from either a fair trade website or a charitable organization. Fair trade websites display merchandise that support good working conditions and salaries for the craftspersons. Usually the fair trade products come from developing countries, and each purchase can help their economy. Charitable organizations sometimes sell commercial beaded chains as fundraisers for the good work they do. Both of these options are generally more expensive than making your own, however. Look through the following websites to find their beaded chains.

Fair Trade Products

- Novica is supported by the National Geographic Society: http://www.novica.com/
- World of Good by ebay displays the work of international fair trade artisans: http://worldofgood.ebay.com/
- Ten Thousand Villages is a fair trade retailer: http://www.tenthousandvillages.com/
- Global Goods Partners strives to change the lives of female artists: http://www.globalgoodspartners.org/
- Outreach Uganda has individual beads and finished products: http://www.outreachuganda.org
- Bead for Life also has loose beads and finished jewelry: http://beadforlifestore.org/
- Fair Trade Designs benefits women and children around the world: http://www.fairtradedesigns.com/

Charitable Organizations in the United States

- Etsy devotes a portion of their website to people who donate a portion of their profits to charity: http://www.etsy.com/search?includes%5B%5D=tags&q=charity+jewelry
- The Greater Good Network supports many different initiatives with their products: https://thehungersite.greatergood.com/
- Unicef offers products to support their efforts to help children: http://www.shopcardsandgifts.unicefusa.org/
- Origami Owl takes many opportunities to give back to those in need. www.origamiowl.com

Make your own Beaded Chain
The best beaded chains come from natural materials
like wood, clay, and paper.

How to Make Paper Beads

Materials needed

Colorful magazine pages or wrapping paper. Thick paper is better.

Pen

Ruler

Toothpick or nail

Tacky glue

Clear nail polish or Mod Podge

Fishing line or the jewelry wire

Directions

1. Cut paper 2" wide by the length of your magazine page or wrapping paper for a slim, oval bead.
2. Cut beads shorter or wider for different shapes. Use a rectangular piece of paper for a tube bead.
3. Starting at the 2" end, roll the paper around the toothpick. Put a dab of glue on the point, and hold until it stays. Leave the bead on the toothpick.
4. Coat beads with nail polish or Mod Podge. Allow to dry. Remove toothpick when dry.
5. String beads on the fishing line or wire. Add smaller space beads between your homemade beads if you want. Attach jewelry clips at the end or tie the strings together.
6. For more information on paper beads, go to http://www.paperbeadcrafts.com/

Other Materials for Beads:

- Polymer clay – follow the directions on the box for molding and baking. You can get many combinations of colors from this craft medium.
- Play dough – you can use commercial or homemade varieties, but keep your beads away from your dog (mine ate a whole necklace because it tasted like a cookie!)
- Aluminum foil – use the traditional paper bead method or crumple it like a ball around a toothpick.
- Seeds and other natural materials that you pierce a hole into with a needle. Be careful! You may need to ask a parent before you use the needle.
- Rose petals – toss lots of rose petals into a blender with ¼ cup of water. Run the blender on high to form a rose paste. Pour into paper towels

and let it drain in the sink until most of the water has dripped through. No matter what color rose petals you use, the paste will always be brown, but it will definitely smell like roses. Roll into balls, insert a toothpick, and allow to dry on newspaper covered with paper towels. (Note: make them slightly larger than you want because they will shrink.)

Final Note

You can certainly purchase individual beads from a craft store for your beaded chain. Pick them out for their specific purposes, rather than simply buying a pre-made beaded chain kit. Take the list of positive personality traits with you as a guide. Then add spacers between the beads for an interesting effect. Be creative with your beaded chain! It can be as short as a bracelet or as long as a necklace. It's your Beaded chain with your thoughts connected to each bead.

You can also make several beaded chains and wear them together or separately for different occasions. Maybe you can even make lots of chains and start your own beaded chain store and spread the message about The Beaded Kingdom and your powerful beaded chain!

Consider starting a Beaded Kingdom club either at school or at home. Make the beads and then discuss what each one means to you. The more you remember about the meaning of each bead, the more your life will improve. Change your thoughts, change your actions, change your life!

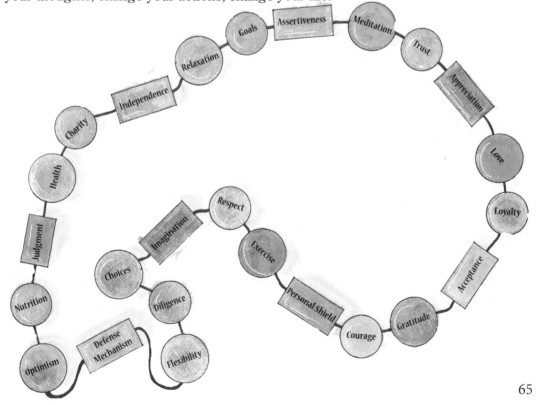

List of Beads to
Make a Full Chain!

About the Author

Renée Heiss is an award-winning educator, author, and co-founder of her own publishing company, Entelechy Education, LLC. She is dedicated to helping young people realize their intellectual, emotional, and moral potential through literature. Find out more about the author at her website, www.reneeheiss.com.

Glossary

abhor: to utterly detest or regard with extreme repugnance

catharsis: the act of relieving emotional tensions

convictions: a fixed or firm belief

demise: the termination of existence or operation

destination wedding: a wedding that takes place in a far away or exotic location

deteriorates: to make worse or inferior in character, quality, value, etc.

elixirs: a medical remedy said to cure any illness

norms: the average or normal performance or expectation

obscure: far from common notice or not well known

philanthropy: engagement or devotion to helping needy people or to other socially useful purposes

sieve: used to sift through something, discarding some parts and keeping others

vulgar: indecent, obscene, or rude

Websites for Brainbuilding

https://www.mensa.org/
http://www.lumosity.com/
http://www.funbrain.com/kidscenter.html
http://www.mindgames.com/brain-games.php
http://www.brainmetrix.com/

Philanthropy Websites and Ideas

http://www.philanthropykids.org/
http://listverse.com/2011/01/27/10-great-philanthropists-who-are-kids/
http://kip.org.au/
http://www.smallfoundations.org/tools-resources/faqs/what-are-some-ways-to-involve-young-children-in-philanthropy/

Websites about Positive Thinking and Self Esteem

http://journalbuddies.com/tag/journal-writing-prompts/
http://positivethinkingradio.com/index.htm
https://www.newmoon.com/
http://www.scouting.org/
http://www.girlscouts.org/

Notes

Notes

Notes

Notes

CPSIA information can be obtained at www.ICGtesting.com
Printed in the USA
LVOW01s2320130514

385552LV00001B/1/P

9 780989 079716